Ball
Field Guide
to Diseases of
Greenhouse Ornamentals

*includes certain problems often
misdiagnosed as contagious diseases*

Margery Daughtrey
A.R. Chase

Ball Publishing

Library of Congress Cataloging-in-Publication Data

Daughtrey, Margery, 1953-
    Ball field guide to diseases of greenhouse ornamentals :
includes certain problems often misdiagnosed as contagious
diseases /Margery Daughtrey, A.R. Chase
        p.   cm.
    Includes bibliographical references (p. 215) and index.
    ISBN 0-9626796-3-1 (soft vinyl cover) :
    1. Greenhouse plants--Diseases and pests--Identification.
2. Plants, Ornamental--Diseases and pests--Identification.
3. Plant diseases--Diagnosis.   I. Chase, A.R. (Ann Renee)
II. Title.
SB608.G82D38   1992
635.9'2--dc20   91-35939
                                                               CIP

Ball Publishing

1 North River Lane
Suite 206
Geneva, Illinois 60134-0532
USA

Contents

Photo contributors

The following generously allowed the use of their photographs in this book. All other photographs were taken by the authors.

Raymond Atilano, photo 450
Minoru Aragaki, photos 18, 20, 21, 453
Larry M. Barnes, photos 25, 115, 277, 346, 347, 497
Gary A. Chastagner, photos 328, 485, 486, 487
Arthur W. Engelhard, photos 376, 377, 380
Mary Francis Heimann, OSF, photo 71
Richard W. Henley, photos 201, 454
Ronald Jones, photos 40, 41, 43, 44, 180, 181, 182
Seong-Hwan Kim, photo 275
Michael LaRocco, photos 81, 82, 257
Leslie MacDonald, photo 447
Maria T. Macksel, photos 17, 242, 259, 391, 422, 435
James A. Matteoni, photos 99, 267
Wayne Nishijima, photo 62
Gail E. Ruhl, photo 313
Charles R. Semer III, photo 100
Gary W. Simone, photos 116, 117, 430
Sherman V. Thomson, photo 339

Introduction

Scout your crops for plant disease symptoms

This book is designed to help greenhouse growers with the challenge of correctly identifying problems that develop in greenhouse foliage and flower crops. Early detection is the most important key to plant disease control: Growers who carefully observe their crop's growth from start to finish—looking for the first signs of contagious disease or cultural problems and responding quickly—will be rewarded by the highest quality finished crops. Prompt response to symptoms observed on just a few plants may allow disease to be rogued out before it spreads throughout the greenhouse and requires pesticide use. If pesticides are required, treatment can be initiated before a full-fledged epidemic develops, thus improving chances for excellent disease control.

Some disease problems occur often enough for growers to become proficient at their diagnoses—while others are rare and difficult to interpret correctly. A laboratory diagnosis will often be necessary in order to choose the proper control action. Plant disease control in the era of integrated pest management requires greenhouse growers to increase their diagnostic skills. A correct diagnosis prevents needless application of inappropriate chemical controls and allows proper choice of cultural and environmental control measures that are able to help keep the diseases problem in check.

The pictures included in this book cannot and should not be used as the sole basis for making a decision on plant disease control. It is intended that they should be a starting point, with a final diagnosis made by a university or private diagnostic laboratory.

What is a plant disease?

The major emphasis in these pages is on contagious diseases caused by infectious microorganisms (called plant pathogens). Some plant injuries caused by insect or mite infestations or by cultural problems have been included because their symptoms are often confused with disease symptoms. Plant diseases may be caused by a number of different pathogen types, including bacteria, fungi, nematodes, viruses, viroids and mycoplasma-like organisms.

When a microorganism is living as a parasite on a living plant, the plant will generally respond with some visible indication of the infection, which we refer to as a disease symptom. Most of the common symptoms caused by plant pathogens are included in this book: leaf spots, flower blights, soft rot, stem cankers, seedling damping-off, root rot, powdery mildew and rust pustules, as well as virus mosaic patterns and ring spots.

In some cases, disease identification is delayed because plant infection is latent within the plant (the pathogen isn't causing any visible effect). Appearance of symptoms may eventually be triggered by more favorable environmental conditions. For this reason, crops must be watched closely for disease symptom development, even if seedlings or cuttings appear to be healthy on receipt from a propagator. Pathogens may also be introduced to a crop any time during production. Poor greenhouse sanitation practices may lead to contamination of growing media, benches, pots or plant parts. Pathogenic microorganisms may linger in the greenhouse between crops within leaf debris on the greenhouse floor, within soil or inside insect vectors or weeds, as well as in or on "pet plants" maintained year-round in the greenhouse. Plant pathogens are easily transmitted from plant to plant by handling, overhead watering or insects.

Infections may be either localized (limited to the visibly affected area) or systemic (throughout conductive systems of the plant, the xylem or phloem). Systemic infections are highly likely to be spread during vegetative propagation. The only way to limit systemic disease spread through the greenhouse industry is establishing culture indexing and virus indexing procedures to supply clean stock for each crop. Indexed stock is currently available for only a few of the more important greenhouse-grown ornamentals, such as geraniums and carnations.

How to use this book

The illustrations in this book are arranged alphabetically by common plant name. If you are interested in learning what effects a particular pathogen might have on a wide range of plants, the index provides a listing of all numbered illustrations in the book showing symptoms caused by that pathogen. Not every plant disease affecting a particular crop is shown, but you will find a high proportion of the common problems pictured within these pages.

If you encounter an unfamiliar term, consult the glossary to gain a better understanding of terms used to describe plant disease symptoms.

Abelmoschus

1 Pseudomonas leaf spot: Spots are angular and have a purplish margin.

Abutilon

2 Cyclamen mite: New leaves are stunted and distorted (compared to a normal leaf).

Aechmea

3 **Helminthosporium leaf spot:** It is more severe on small plants since spots coalesce.

Aeschynanthus

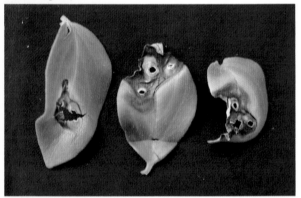

4 **Corynespora leaf spot:** Sunken areas contribute to leaf distortion.

5 **Pythium cutting rot:** Roots and stems turn mushy and collapse.

6 Rhizoctonia aerial blight: Dense mat of brown webs forms on plant surfaces.

7 Botrytis blight: It affects cutting bases, especially under high humidity.

Aglaonema

8 Copper toxicity: Spots form anywhere on leaves and are initially water-soaked with a yellow halo.

Aglaonema

9 **Xanthomonas blight:** Lesions are water-soaked and have a yellow halo.

10 Dasheen mosaic virus: Leaves show color breaking and slight distortion.

11 Fusarium root and stem rot: Plants
have mushy stem rot and lose roots
and lower leaves.

12 Myrothecium leaf spot: Spots start at
leaf wound sites.

Aglaonema

13 Erwinia blight: Leaves disintegrate and sometimes smell rotten.

14 Chilling injury: Grayish-brown water-soaking occurs after as little as four hours' exposure to 50 F.

15 **Nitrogen deficiency:** Plants have poor growth and pale green color.

16 **Bent-tip:** Leaves fail to separate from the leaf sheath and are permanently bent or become torn (the cause remains unknown).

Anemone

17 **Tomato spotted wilt virus:** Chlorotic leaf patches turn necrotic.

Anthurium

18 **Anthracnose:** Tiny black spots form on the spadix.

19 **Copper toxicity:** Spots are pale-colored and sometimes slightly raised.

20 Phytophthora leaf spot: Leaves have dark brown to black spots.

21 Phytophthora flower blight: Spots are black and may cover the whole flower.

Anthurium

22 Pythium root rot: You can easily pull outer root layers away from the inner core.

23 Xanthomonas blight: Spots appear on leaf margins, surrounded by a yellow halo.

Aphelandra

24 **Corynespora leaf spot:** Black or dark brown spots form on leaf tips and margins in contact with the potting medium.

25 Tomato spotted wilt virus: Leaves show brown veinal necrosis.

Aphelandra

26 **Phytophthora stem rot:** Mushy black rot at the soil line causes stem collapse.

27 **Nitrogen deficiency:** New leaves are pale green and stunted.

28 **Myrothecium leaf spot:** Spots enlarge and kill small cuttings.

Araucaria

29 Anthracnose: Needles on branch tips are brown and may mat together.

Begonia

30 Fusarium stem rot: Stem lesions form at the soil line, causing a dry rot.

Begonia

31 **Myrothecium leaf spot:** Spots form at wound sites.

32 **Botrytis blight:** Water-soaked lesions turn brown and zonate over time.

33 Bacterial leaf spot: Spots form all over leaves. Spots are sometimes confined between veins on a Rex begonia (*B. rex*).

34 Bacterial leaf spot: Small, round, purple spots appear on a Nonstop begonia (*B.* x *tuberhybrida*).

35 Bacterial leaf spot: V-shaped wedges of dead tissue form on a Rieger begonia (*B. socatrana* x *tuberhybrida*).

Begonia

36 Bacterial leaf spot: Infected begonias may collapse completely in hot weather.

37 Powdery mildew: Early stage of infection on a Rieger begonia (*B. socatrana* x *tuberhybrida*) has small, separate fungal colonies.

38 Powdery mildew: Extensive fungal growth and spore chains typically give leaves a powdery, white coating.

39 Powdery mildew: Dark, bruised-looking areas not showing extensive white fungus growth may be mistaken for other injury.

40 Tomato spotted wilt virus: Leaves have mottling, spotting and ringspots, as well as vein discoloration.

41 Tomato spotted wilt virus: Darkened vein sections are best viewed from leaf undersides.

Begonia

42 Tomato spotted wilt virus: New growth on Rieger begonia (*B. socatrana* x *tuberhybrida*) is severely stunted and has chlorotic mottling.

43 Tomato spotted wilt virus: Wax begonia (*B. semperflorens*) has brown line patterns in foliage.

44 Tomato spotted wilt virus: Wax begonia (*B. semperflorens*) leaves have brown patches at the petiole end.

45 Broad mite: Leaves have bronzed interveinal areas on undersides.

Bougainvillea

46 **Pseudomonas leaf spot:** Leaves have roughly circular dark spots, usually with a reddish-brown margin.

Browallia

47 **Pythium damping-off:** Plug flats have poor seedling germination.

Cacti and Succulents

48 **Dichotomophthora spot:** Opuntia has dark and sunken lesions.

49 **Helminthosporium stem rot:** Opuntia shows black lesions.

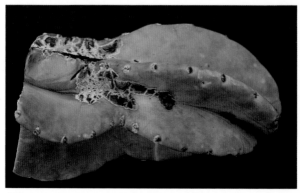

50 **Helminthosporium stem rot:** Cereus has corky, dry lesions.

Cacti and Succulents

51 **Helminthosporium blight:** Easter cactus foliage is shattered with sunken, circular lesions.

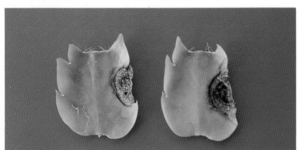

52 **Helminthosporium blight:** Christmas cactus has sunken lesions with a black coating of fungal spores.

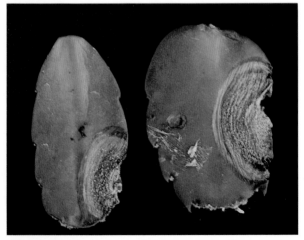

53 **Fusarium stem rot:** Christmas cactus has concentric patterns in lesions covered with ochre-colored fungal spores.

54 **Fusarium stem rot:** Basal segment of
Christmas cactus completely decays.

55 **Erwinia blight:** Easter cactus collapses.

Cacti and Succulents

56 Erwinia blight: *Aloe vera* shows a wet rot.

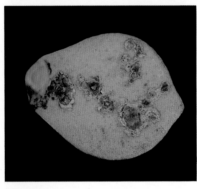

57 Fusarium: Crassula leaves have corky spots.

Calathea

58 Fusarium wilt: Leaves die due to vascular infection.

59 **Helminthosporium leaf spot:** Large, dead, brown spots form on leaves still in the whorl.

60 **Alternaria leaf spot:** Leaves have small, reddish spots rarely exceeding one-eighth-inch diameter.

61 Cucumber mosaic virus: Mosaic patterns are hard to detect on most calatheas.

62 Foliar nematode: Leaves have large, brown areas often vein-delimited.

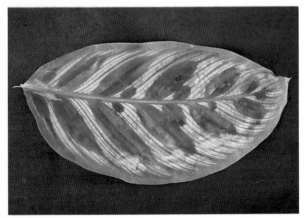

63 Fluoride damage: Leaves have marginal injury.

64 Pseudomonas leaf spot: Very large, papery lesions are initially greasy-looking (under wet conditions).

65 High soluble salts: Marginal burn is frequently found on leaf tips.

Calendula

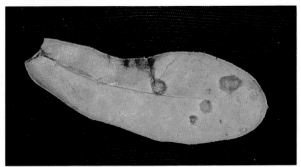

66 Smut: Leaves have rounded brown spots.

Calla Lily

67 **Bacterial stem rot:** Stem bases show soft, brown decay.

68 **Virus:** Leaves show chlorotic mottling.

China Aster

69 **Rust:** Small yellow spots appear on upper leaf surfaces.

70 **Rust:** Pustules containing yellow-orange spores are on leaf undersides.

71 **Aster yellows:** Stunted plants have yellowed foliage.

China Aster

72 Aster yellows: Flowers are virescent (green).

Chrysanthemum

73 Fusarium wilt: Plants show stunting, scorching, chlorosis and wilting (water stress symptoms).

74 Fusarium wilt: Sometimes plants show a one-sided effect.

75 Bacterial leaf spot: Black spots are irregularly-shaped when actively expanding.

76 Bacterial leaf spot: Spots turn from black to brown when they dry.

77 Bacterial leaf spot: Flower buds may have blight.

Chrysanthemum

78 Bacterial leaf spot: Flower bud blight may be extensive.

79 Bacterial leaf spot: Pedicels may turn brown, causing flowers to droop.

80 Bacterial leaf spot: Infected stem portions blacken.

81 White rust: Leaves have pale, round spots.

Chrysanthemum

82 White rust: Leaf undersides have pale pustules.

83 Rust: Brown spots with yellow halo appear on leaves.

84 Rust: Older round, brown sunken spots appear on upper leaf surfaces.

85 Rust: Brown, powdery spore pustules appear at center of spots on leaf undersides.

Chrysanthemum

86 Foliar nematode: Young leaves show distortion.

87 Foliar nematode: Here is a closeup of distorted leaf surfaces.

88 Foliar nematode: Brown, dead areas form on leaves, beginning with lowest leaves and progressing upward.

89 Crown gall: Callus-like growths form at wounds (most often at cutting bases or on roots).

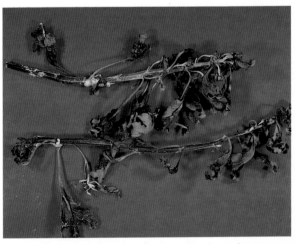

90 Sclerotinia blight: A thick, white fungal mat forms on a brown, cankered stem base.

Chrysanthemum

91 **Tomato spotted wilt virus:** Stem has brown, dead sections.

92 **Tomato spotted wilt virus:** Leaves in the area of a stem canker turn brown from the petiole end.

93 Tomato spotted wilt virus: Infected stems may eventually wilt.

Cineraria

94 Alternaria leaf spot: Leaves have small, brown spots with purple margins.

95 Tomato spotted wilt virus: Leaves have small, round, yellow spots.

96 Tomato spotted wilt virus: Foliage becomes yellow-mottled in a systemic infection.

97 **Tomato spotted wilt virus:** Symptoms often show only on a few older leaves.

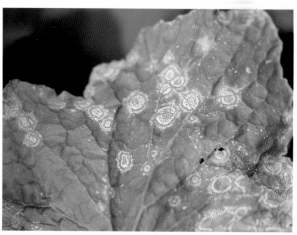

98 **Tomato spotted wilt virus:** Concentric ring patterns of white or brown (ring spots) may appear on older leaves.

Cineraria

99 **Tomato spotted wilt virus:** Leaf petiole and veins have black sections.

Cissus

100 **Cylindrocladium cutting rot:** Cutting bases show a dry rot.

101 Powdery mildew: White masses of spores cover leaves of infected plants.

102 Powdery mildew: Young leaves are stunted and distorted.

103 Anthracnose: Leaf spots have concentric patterns of light and dark tissue.

Cissus

104 **Anthracnose:** Expansion between veins causes windowpane effect.

105 **Botrytis blight:** Cuttings collapse completely.

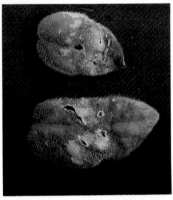

Columnea

106 **Corynespora leaf spot:** Spots are usually dry and form at wound sites.

107 Rhizoctonia aerial blight: Leaf drop occurs on some plants.

Cordyline

108 Cercospora leaf spot: Spots appear similar to Phyllosticta leaf spot.

Cordyline

109 **Phyllosticta leaf spot:** Expansion between veins causes windowpane spots.

110 **Phyllosticta leaf spot:** Lesions are similar to those caused by fluoride damage but are usually more circular and appear anywhere on the leaf.

111 Fluoride damage: Leaf tips are brown and have chlorotic margins.

112 Southern blight: Cutting bases show a wet rot.

Cordyline

113 Erwinia stem rot: Leaf base shows a wet rot.

114 Fusarium root rot: Roots turn dark brown.

Crossandra

115 Black root rot: Roots are black in Thielaviopsis infection.

Croton

116 Crown gall: Corky galls form on wounded stem areas.

Croton

117 Crown gall: Sometimes galls form on wounded leaves.

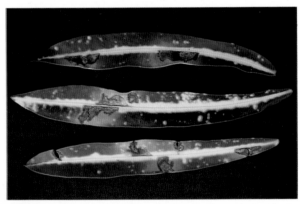

118 Xanthomonas leaf spot: Leaves have irregularly shaped, brown lesions with raised margins.

119 Xanthomonas leaf spot: Leaf undersides have obvious, water-soaked lesions.

Cyclamen

120 **Botrytis blight:** Petiole bases rot and may cause portions of the plant to collapse.

121 **Bacterial soft rot:** Entire plant wilts.

Cyclamen

122 **Bacterial soft rot:** Corms turn soft and mushy.

123 **Fusarium wilt:** Leaves progressively yellow and wilt.

124 Fusarium wilt: Corm cross-sections show reddish-purple to brown discoloration in the vascular system.

125 Fusarium wilt: Seedlings yellow and wilt.

126 Fusarium wilt: Seedling has root rot.

Cyclamen

127 **Fusarium wilt:** Young transplants wilt.

128 **Deep planting:** Potting corms too deeply can predispose plants to diseases such as bacterial soft rot.

129 Cylindrocarpon rot: Petioles show brown rot at their bases and leaves wilt.

130 Black vine weevil: Wilting plants may result from larvae of the black vine weevil feeding just beneath the corm.

131 Tomato spotted wilt virus: Leaves have round, brown spots and ring spots.

Cyclamen

132 Tomato spotted wilt virus: Foliage may show a brown line pattern.

Dahlia

133 Smut: Leaves show light brown, round spots with pale halos.

134 Smut: Lesion closeup.

135 Botrytis blight: Brown, irregularly-shaped spots may show a yellow halo.

136 Tomato spotted wilt virus: Leaves have chlorotic zigzag patterns and ring spots.

Dianthus

137 Fusarium wilt: Portions of plant yellow and wilt.

138 Fusarium wilt: Plants in a large portion of the bench brown and wilt.

139 Alternaria leaf spot: Leaves show small purple spots with associated yellowing.

140 Alternaria leaf spot: Leaf spot closeup.

141 Rust: Leaves have yellow spots containing brown spore pustules.

Dianthus

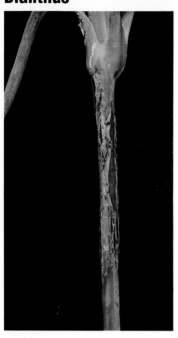

142 **Rust:** Stems may also have brown spore pustules.

143 Rhizoctonia: Stem bases have brown cankers.

Dieffenbachia

144 **Dasheen mosaic virus:** Bausei cultivar is so sensitive to the virus that infection results in death.

145 **Dasheen mosaic virus:** Perfection cultivar shows mosaic pattern on leaves.

Dieffenbachia

146 **Dasheen mosaic virus:** *D. amoena* shows color break and slight distortion.

147 **Dasheen mosaic virus:** Rudolph Roehrs cultivar gets dark green ringspots.

148 **Copper toxicity:** Leaves get
somewhat sunken, necrotic speckles.

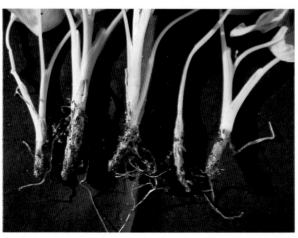

149 **Fusarium stem rot:** Roots rot and stems become
mushy.

Dieffenbachia

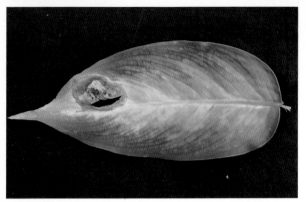

150 **Fusarium leaf spot:** Leaves show large, papery necrotic spots.

151 **Pythium root rot:** Roots die completely due to advanced rot.

152 Sunburn damage: Exposed leaves show papery, dry areas.

153 Cold damage: Entire plant shows extensive tissue collapse one week after exposure.

Dieffenbachia

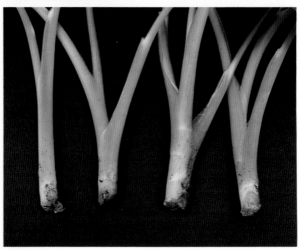

154 Erwinia stem rot: Cuttings become mushy and rot and a rotten, fishy odor may be present.

155 Myrothecium leaf spot: Leaves have circular spots with fruiting bodies in centers.

156 Leptosphaeria leaf spot: Small dark-rimmed spots with yellow halos contain fungal spore bodies.

157 Xanthomonas blight: Leaves show severe blight with bright yellow margins.

Dieffenbachia

158 Anthracnose: Concentric rings of light and dark brown contain black spore bodies of the fungus.

Dracaena

159 Fusarium leaf spot: Reddish lesions with yellow halos first appear on younger leaves.

160 **Fusarium leaf spot:** Severe infections can result in plant loss.

161 **Fusarium stem rot:** Stem dry rots. Fusarium rot can be easily confused with Erwinia stem rot on dracaenas.

Dracaena

162 **Erwinia stem rot:** Stem tissue is
   smelly, mushy and commonly
   appears wet.

163 **Erwinia leaf spot:** Spots form on leaf margins
   and tips and can be either dry or wet, depending
   upon conditions.

164 Anthracnose: Spots form on lower leaves first.

165 Foliar discoloration: Foliage color loss can be due to a root rot disease or nutritional imbalance.

Dracaena

166 Cold damage: Irregularly-shaped, dead areas appear along leaf margins.

167 Botrytis blight: Lower leaves in contact with potting medium die.

168 Fluoride damage: Reddish brown, elliptical lesions form in the white tissue of cultivar Warneckii.

169 Speckling: Light yellow areas appear in leaf tips (cause is unknown).

Dracaena

170 Calcium deficiency: Notches form on leaf edges close to stems.

Dusty Miller

171 Alternaria leaf spot: Leaves get brown spots; stems damp off.

172 **Alternaria leaf spot:** Irregularly-shaped brown leaf lesion closeup.

Euphorbia
(for *Euphorbia pulcherrima*, see Poinsettia)

173 **Phytophthora stem rot:** Wet, mushy stem rot starts at stem base and moves upward.

Euphorbia

(for *Euphorbia pulcherrima*, see Poinsettia)

174 Phomopsis blight: Stems or leaves show dry, corky, irregularly-shaped lesions.

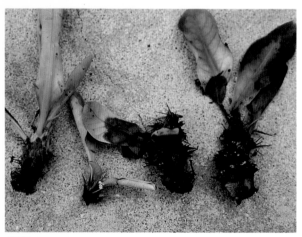

175 Erwinia stem rot: Mushy, wet stem rot extends from stem base into tops of cuttings.

176 Rhizopus stem rot: Wet stem rot is accompanied by furry, black, fungal mycelia.

Exacum

177 Botrytis blight: Leaves show tan to gray-ish spots.

178 Botrytis stem canker: Stem cankers cause wilting, which can be confused with tomato spotted wilt virus infections.

179 **Botrytis:** Stem base shows canker.

180 **Tomato spotted wilt virus:** Portions of branches turn tan and collapse.

181 **Tomato spotted wilt virus:** Collapsed branch section and main stem canker closeup.

182 **Tomato spotted wilt virus:** Stems get dark cankers.

Fatsia

183 Alternaria leaf spot: Leaves get large black lesions, up to 2 inches in diameter.

184 Fusarium stem rot: Seedlings wilt and stems rot.

185 Xanthomonas blight: Leaves show margin infection with yellow, vein-delimited spots.

186 Pseudomonas leaf spot: Dry, papery, tan lesions can run along veins.

Fern

187 Rhizoctonia aerial blight: Rabbit's foot fern blackens at the crown.

188 Rhizoctonia aerial blight: Reddish-brown mycelia cover fronds of asparagus fern.

189 **Rhizoctonia aerial blight:** Boston fern shows black, water-soaked spots in the crown.

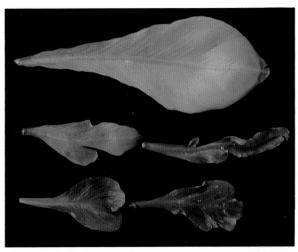

190 **Nitrogen toxicity:** New leaves severely distort on bird's nest fern.

Fern

191 Pseudomonas leaf spot: Table ferns show red-brown spots with irregular shapes.

192 Pseudomonas leaf spot: Brown leaf areas are easily confused with foliar nematode on bird's nest fern.

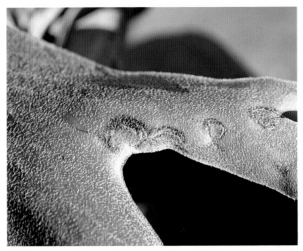

193 **Pseudomonas leaf spot:** Roughly circular, brown spots on staghorn fern can be confused with Rhizoctonia leaf spots.

194 **Myrothecium leaf spot:** Spots are gray to black and contain the black and white sporodochia of the fungus.

Fern

195 Bendiocarb phytotoxicity: Frond tips turn tan.

Ficus

196 Botrytis blight: During cutting shipment, large areas of wet rot appear covered with grayish-brown fungal spores.

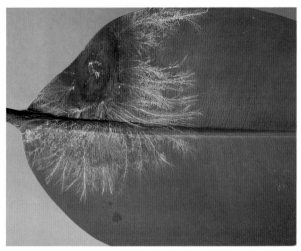

197 Southern blight: Leaves have tan to white, fan-like fungal growth.

198 Southern blight: Infection of the center of a creeping ficus causes browning and general rot.

Ficus

199 Phomopsis dieback: Twig death with or without leaf loss usually occurs on indoor plants only.

200 Phomopsis dieback: Slicing into large stems shows the dark line of fungal growth in the wood.

201 Bendiocarb phytotoxicity: Drench application results in spots often confused with anthracnose disease.

202 Myrothecium leaf spot: Papery brown spots appear at wound sites.

203 Xanthomonas leaf spot: Pinpoint lesions can coalesce and cause severe yellowing and leaf drop.

204 Pseudomonas leaf spot: Infections start at the petiole end of fiddle-leaf fig leaves.

Ficus

205 Crown gall: Corky, dry galls form at wounded areas.

206 Foliar nematode: Browned leaf areas are usually vein-delimited.

207 **Cuban laurel thrips:** Leaves curl shut and become severely distorted.

208 **Anthracnose:** Spots are brown to black and coalesce to destroy large leaf areas.

Fittonia

209 **Xanthomonas blight:** Browning of white tissue portions along veins is common.

210 **Biden's mottle virus:** New leaves are distorted.

211 Chilling injury: White to tan speckles form all over leaf surfaces.

Freesia

212 Fluoride toxicity: The streaked plant is growing in a low pH medium, which causes excess availability of fluoride.

Fuchsia

213 Botrytis blight: The fungus will sporulate on leaf spots.

214 Botrytis blight: Stem cankers may cause branches to wilt.

215 Rust: Leaf spotting usually shows on only a few leaves.

216 Rust: Spots have tan centers and purple borders.

217 Rust: Apricot-colored spores appear on leaf undersides.

218 Thielaviopsis root rot: Root tips are quite black, darker than a typical Pythium infection.

Fuchsia

219 **Thielaviopsis root rot:** Roots blacken.

220 **Thielaviopsis root rot:** Plants wilt due to extensive root decay.

221 **Cyclamen mite:** New growth is stunted and curled.

Geranium *(Pelargonium)*

222 Alternaria leaf spot: Sunken brown, zonate spots are generally larger than those caused by Xanthomonas.

223 Pseudomonas leaf spot: Spots are initially black, becoming tan and sunken as they dry.

224 Bacterial fasciation: Clumps of stunted, misshapen shoots appear at plant base.

Geranium *(Pelargonium)*

225 Bacterial blight: Ivy geranium shows leaf spots.

226 Bacterial blight: Lower leaves may turn brown on infected ivy geraniums.

227 Bacterial blight: Ivy geranium also shows systemic infection symptoms.

228 Bacterial blight: Zonal geraniums may show small, round, brown leaf spots (one-sixteenth to one-eighth inch in diameter).

229 Bacterial blight: Individual leaf spots may coalesce on zonal geraniums.

230 Bacterial blight: Zonal geraniums may show brown leaf spots and wedges with yellow halos.

Geranium *(Pelargonium)*

231 Bacterial blight: Leaves may show round patterns within dead brown wedges, as well as scattered individual spots.

232 Bacterial blight: Lower leaves wilt and yellow due to systemic infection.

233 Bacterial blight: Zonal geraniums may show only a single wilted leaf.

234 Bacterial blight: Seedling geraniums may show yellow, wilting and brown leaves.

Geranium *(Pelargonium)*

235 **Bacterial blight:** Black stem cankers sometimes form at the branch bases on stock plants.

236 **Bacterial blight:** Internal stem tissue discolors darkly in advanced infections.

237 Rhizoctonia damping-off: Geranium cuttings show a poor seedling stand in contaminated flats.

238 Rhizoctonia damping-off: Roots decay; stems rot at the soil line.

Geranium *(Pelargonium)*

239 **Cylindrocladium stem canker:** Stem portions turn brown.

240 **Fusarium root rot:** Root infection causes above-ground wilting.

241 Fusarium root rot: Root system turns dark from decay.

242 Iron-manganese toxicity: Leaves show scattered, brown flecks, chlorosis and marginal scorch.

243 Fungus gnats and Pythium root rot: Roots decay; larval feeding increases fungal injury.

Geranium *(Pelargonium)*

244 Verticillium wilt: Leaves yellow and wilt.

245 Pythium damping-off: Stem bases of young seedling geraniums turn black.

246 Pythium root and stem rot: A black canker and a mass of fungal mycelia appear at the stem base of a seed geranium.

247 Pythium root and stem rot: Lower leaves on Regal (Martha Washington) geraniums yellow and wilt.

248 Botrytis blight: The fungus will sporulate on senescent flowers.

Geranium *(Pelargonium)*

249 **Botrytis blight:** Flowers get blight symptoms, too.

250 **Botrytis blight:** Zonate, brown leaf lesions may sporulate.

251 Botrytis blight: Lower leaves yellow and rot.

252 Botrytis blight: Spores may cover stem cankers.

Geranium *(Pelargonium)*

253 **Rhizopus:** Seedlings may die.

254 **Rust:** Small, round yellow spots show on upper leaf surfaces.

255 Rust: Reddish-brown, powdery spore pustules form on leaf undersides opposite the yellow spots on upper surfaces.

256 Rust: Spore pustules form concentric rings on leaf undersides.

Geranium *(Pelargonium)*

257 Rust: Leaves exposed to rain show bright yellow spots.

258 Virus: Chlorotic patterns indicate infection by one or more viruses.

259 **High soluble salts:** Leaves show edge necrosis and interveinal chlorosis.

260 **Oedema:** Corky, tan blisterings appear on leaf undersides of ivy geraniums. Spider mite feeding may look similar.

Gerbera

261 Thrips: Feeding causes white streaking and petal distortion.

262 Leaf miner: Leaf blotches may resemble fungal spots.

263 Cyclamen mite: New growth is dark and distorted.

264 Pythium root rot: Purple foliage indicates poor nutrient uptake by the damaged root system.

265 Botrytis blight: Flower petals show blight symptoms.

Gerbera

266 Powdery mildew: Patches of whitish fungal growth appear on upper leaf surfaces.

267 Tomato spotted wilt virus: Red lines show along leaf veins.

268 Pseudomonas leaf spot: Tan spots may form at wounds and rapidly enlarge along leaf veins.

269 **Rhizopus blight:** Leaves may turn black and become covered with fuzzy, black and gray fungus.

270 **Rhizopus blight:** Flower petals turn brown.

Gerbera

271 Rhizopus blight: Infected flowers can become mummified in fungal mycelia.

272 Iron deficiency: Stunted leaves develop severe interveinal yellowing.

273 Iron toxicity: Leaf margins turn brown; new leaves are severely stunted.

Gloxinia (Sinningia)

274 **Myrothecium stem rot:** Large plants may suddenly wilt and die due to stem cankers near the soil line.

275 Phytophthora crown rot: Young leaves are brown and dead.

276 **Tomato spotted wilt virus:** Brown, dead young leaves at center of plant similar to Phytophthora crown rot.

Gloxinia (Sinningia)

277 Tomato spotted wilt virus: Leaves show vein necrosis and ringspots.

278 Tomato spotted wilt virus: Leaf spots are brown and round.

Hedera

279 Pythium root rot: Lower leaves wilt due to water loss.

280 Rhizoctonia leaf spot: Discrete dry spots appear near center of plant.

281 Rhizoctonia leaf spot: Closeup of active spots shows wet appearance.

282 Chlorothalonil phytotoxicity: Small, brown spots appear on leaves.

Hedera

283 **Streptomycin sulfate phytotoxicity:** Leaves show severe chlorosis.

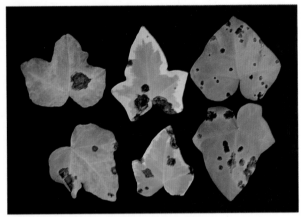

284 **Xanthomonas leaf spot:** It's easy to confuse these roughly circular black spots with those caused by anthracnose fungi.

285 **Anthracnose:** Black spots with yellow halos are sometimes confused with Xanthomonas leaf spot.

286 **Botrytis blight:** Cutting rot often occurs.

287 **Broad mite:** New growth is stunted.

Hibiscus

288 *Pseudomonas cichorii* **leaf spot:** Large, irregularly-shaped spots with purplish margins and yellow halos develop during moderate temperatures.

Hibiscus

289 *Pseudomonas syringae* **leaf spot:** Small, pinpoint lesions causing new leaf distortion occur during cooler temperatures.

290 Xanthomonas leaf spot: Spots are vein-delimited with a yellow halo and occur during warm weather.

291 **Cercospora leaf spot:** This fungal infection looks similar to Xanthomonas leaf spot.

Impatiens

292 **Rhizoctonia stem rot:** Plants collapse completely from stem lesions.

Impatiens

293 Rhizoctonia damping-off: Leaves mat down on collapsed plants.

294 Pseudomonas leaf spot: Reddish-purple spots may have white to tan clear areas in their centers.

295 Pseudomonas leaf spot: Water-soaked spots are vein-delimited on New Guinea impatiens.

296 Ethylene injury: Meristem of young seedlings is stunted.

297 Cyclamen mite: Young growth curls and could be mistaken for a viral infection.

127

Impatiens

298 **Rhizoctonia stem rot:** Brown stem cankers show cobweb-like strands of tan mycelia.

299 **Pythium root rot:** New Guinea impatiens with black lines at stem bases and discolored roots.

300 **Tomato spotted wilt virus:** Scattered, small black leaf spots appear on double-flowered impatiens.

301 Tomato spotted wilt virus: Tiny, black, irregularly-shaped spots may have tan centers.

302 Tomato spotted wilt virus: Black spotting occurs at petiole ends of New Guinea impatiens leaves.

303 Tomato spotted wilt virus: Only a few leaves per plant may show ringspot symptoms.

Impatiens

304 Tomato spotted wilt virus: Double flowered impatiens leaves may be mottled yellow.

305 Tomato spotted wilt virus: Stem sections turn black.

306 Tomato spotted wilt virus: Leaves abscise in blackened stem section.

307 **Tomato spotted wilt virus:** Brown ringspots may appear on leaves.

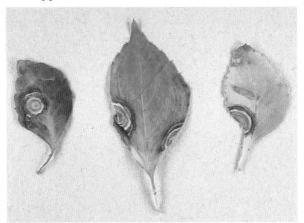

308 **Tomato spotted wilt virus:** Target-like ringspots may appear on leaves.

309 **Tomato spotted wilt virus:** Yellowing is associated with leaf ringspots.

Impatiens

310 **Tomato spotted wilt virus:** Zonate leaf spots appear on New Guinea impatiens.

311 **Tomato spotted wilt virus:** Distorted, blistered and mottled foliage appears on New Guinea impatiens.

312 **Broad mite:** Leaves are stunted and edges curl under.

313 **Dodder:** A yellow stem with small white flower clusters parasitizes impatiens stems.

Impatiens

314 **Botrytis blight:** Tiny round spots appear on petals.

315 **Botrytis blight:** Tiny round spots appear on petals.

Kalanchoe

316 Rhizoctonia aerial blight: The fungus shows as a brown web, matting leaves to soil.

317 Rhizopus blight: Stem cankers cause portions of plant to collapse.

Kalanchoe

318 **Rhizopus blight:** Stem canker closeup.

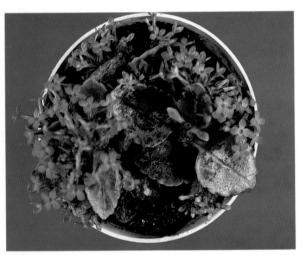

319 **Powdery mildew:** Bronze patches may resemble pesticide toxicity.

320 Powdery mildew: Bronze patch closeup.

321 Botrytis: Lower leaves may die.

Leea

322 **Calonectria stem rot:** Lower stem is cankered; leaves drop.

323 **Phytophthora damping-off:** Poor seed germination occurs.

324 **Xanthomonas leaf spot:** Brown spots with reddish margins are scattered across leaves.

Liatris

325 **Rhizoctonia stem and bulb rot:** Infected plants show stunting and wilting due to stem cankers (healthy plant on left).

Lily

326 Pythium root rot: Outer (cortical) root tissue turns soft, brown and mushy as it decays.

327 Botrytis blight: Petals show blight symptoms.

328 Botrytis blight: Brown, elliptical lesions appear on leaves.

329 Sclerotinia blight: Petals show small, brown spots.

Lisianthus

330 Botrytis blight: Stem cankers appear near soil line.

Lisianthus

331 **Botrytis blight:** Plants may wilt due to stem base cankers.

332 **Botrytis blight:** Tan cankers occur at cutting stubs.

Maranta

333 **Pythium root rot:** Leaves yellow and die due to root rot.

334 **Helminthosporium leaf spot:** Tan, circular spots of all sizes are scattered across leaves.

Maranta

335 **Cucumber mosaic virus:** Yellow mosaic patterns appear at leaf bases.

336 **Cucumber mosaic virus:** Yellow zig-zag patterns appear in leaf centers.

337 **Benomyl phytotoxicity:** Plants show degrees of stunting and yellowing.

Marigold

338 **Iron-manganese toxicity:** Leaves have inter-veinal yellowing, dark flecking and stunting compared to healthy plants grown at a higher pH.

339 **Sclerotinia stem canker:** White cottony mycelia and black resistant structures called sclerotia form on stem bases of wilted plants.

Marigold

340 Botrytis blight: Tan stem cankers form under poor air circulation, progressing from leaf infections.

341 Pythium root rot: Root rot progresses into stem cankers and may kill plants (as in the patch of infected plants at center).

146

342 Alternaria leaf spot: Stem lesions may girdle young plants.

Orchid

343 Virus: Black markings resembling fungal or bacterial leaf spots may indicate viral infection.

344 Odontoglossum ringspot virus: *Chysis aurea* shows brown spots.

Pansy

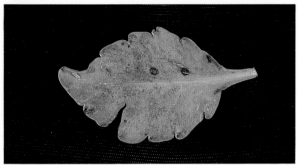

345 **Mycocentrospora leaf spot:** Leaves have round, purple spots.

346 **Thielaviopsis root rot:** Plants show progressive stunting, leaf yellowing and black root rot.

347 **Thielaviopsis root rot:** Closeup comparing healthy and diseased roots.

Pellionia

348 **Xanthomonas leaf spot:** Dryish, corky, irregularly-shaped brown spots appear on leaves.

349 **Myrothecium leaf spot:** Leaf undersides show fungal sporodochia in concentric rings within the spot.

Peperomia

350 Virus: Round, brown patterns appear on leaves.

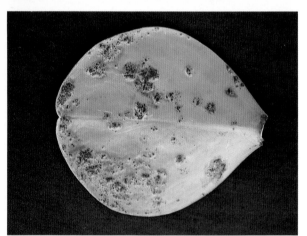

351 Cercospora leaf spot: Raised, brown, corky areas on lower leaf surfaces are sometimes confused with oedema.

352 Myrothecium leaf spot: Wound sites show round lesions.

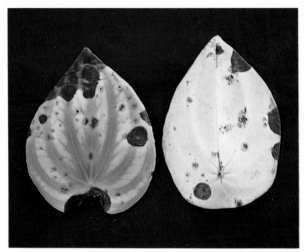

353 **Phyllostictina leaf spot:** Sunken, round, black spots may appear all over leaf surfaces of watermelon peperomia.

354 **Pythium root rot:** Young rubber tree plants may be stunted compared to healthy plants.

Peperomia

355 **Rhizoctonia leaf spot:** Leaves show concentric rings of light and dark tissue within spots. Sclerotia (roundish tan bumps) appear within spots.

356 **Phytophthora stem rot:** Wet, mushy stem rot at soil line results in cutting loss.

Pepper

357 Tomato spotted wilt virus: Black markings on leaves are concentrated at petiole end.

358 Xanthomonas leaf spot: Leaves have tan spots with purple borders.

Petunia

359 Sclerotinia stem canker: White cottony mycelia and black sclerotia develop on infected seedling stems.

360 Rhizoctonia: Basal stem canker causes lower leaf drop.

Petunia

361 **Rhizoctonia:** Lower leaves collapse.

Philodendron

362 **Dactylaria leaf spot:** Blister-like, raised yellow spots appear on heartleaf philodendron.

363 Red-edge or Xanthomonas blight:
Heartleaf philodendron leaves have
reddish leaf edges, water-soaking
and early chlorosis.

364 Rhizoctonia aerial blight: Mycelia masses form
reddish-brown spiderwebs.

Philodendron

365 **Rhizoctonia leaf spot:** Discrete reddish spots with water-soaked margins appear on leaves.

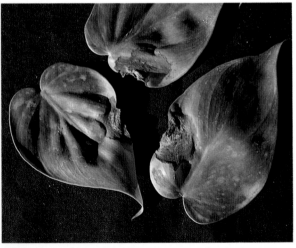

366 **Phytophthora leaf spot:** Large, dry lesions start on leaf edges.

367 **Southern blight:** Leaf rot can occur in stock beds.

368 **Erwinia blight:** Leaves have wet spots with concentric rings.

Philodendron

369 Erwinia blight: Inactive leaf spots also show concentric rings.

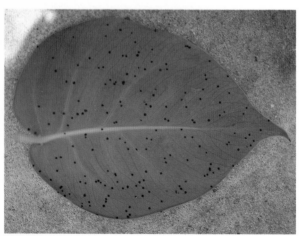

370 Crucibulum (bird's nest fungus): Fruiting bodies appear on philodendron leaves.

371 **Crucibulum (bird's nest fungus):** Fruiting bodies closeup.

Pilea

372 **Rhizoctonia aerial blight:** Moon Valley pilea cuttings collapse.

373 **Xanthomonas blight:** Aluminum plants show white tissue disintegration.

Pilea

374 Xanthomonas blight: Black, angular lesions appear on leaves.

Poinsettia *(Euphorbia pulcherrima)*

375 Scab: Scab-like, tan lesions form on leaves, petioles and stems.

376 Scab: Raised leaf lesions may show yellow halos.

377 Scab: White scabby areas may be extensive on stems.

Poinsettia *(Euphorbia pulcherrima)*

378 Corynespora spot: Only bracts appear to develop the black to brown spots on their margins.

379 Xanthomonas leaf spot: Angular, brown lesions with bright yellow halos may be pinpoint to one-fourth inch in diameter.

380 **Alternaria leaf spot:** Leaves show small spots, vein necrosis and blight.

381 **Botrytis blight:** Light tan stem cankers appear on poorly-aerated stock plants.

Poinsettia *(Euphorbia pulcherrima)*

382 Botrytis blight: Cankers may form on main stem of a poinsettia "tree."

383 Rhizoctonia stem rot: Cutting bases turn brown.

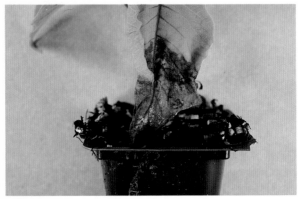

384 Rhizoctonia leaf spot: Large, brown dead areas appear on leaves in contact with the soil.

385 Rhizopus stem rot: Dark, greasy-looking stem cankers develop under moist conditions.

386 Rhizopus blight: Stem infections can lead to wilting and plant death.

Poinsettia *(Euphorbia pulcherrima)*

387 **Thielaviopsis root rot:** Stem base of a wilted plant shows vertical cracks.

388 **Thielaviopsis root rot:** Fungal resting spores may blacken stem bases.

389 **Aerosol injury:** Overly close placement of an aerosol causes white bract markings.

390 Bacterial soft rot: Lower portions of cuttings soften and collapse.

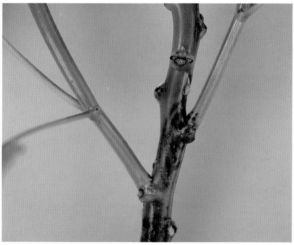

391 Chlorine bleach injury: Concentric black ring patterns appear at stem nodes.

Poinsettia *(Euphorbia pulcherrima)*

392 Chlorine bleach injury: Stems show black, zonate lesions and dark flecks.

393 Fusarium stem rot: Infected cuttings wilt.

394 Pythium root rot: Rooted cuttings wilt.

395 Pythium root and stem rot: Dark stem lesions follow root rot.

396 Mechanical injury: Branches wilt.

Poinsettia *(Euphorbia pulcherrima)*

397 Bacterial wilt: During hot weather, plants collapse and stems are soft and sticky.

398 Phytophthora wilt: Stock plants may have a single wilted branch.

399 Phytophthora wilt: Shoot tips blacken; leaves brown and die.

400 Phytophthora wilt: Cankers may form at cutting bases with a black line running up the stem.

Polyscias

401 **Cercospora leaf spot:** Large, diffuse yellow areas are visible on upper leaf surfaces.

402 Anthracnose: Various types of spots form, primarily starting on leaf margins.

403 Pseudomonas leaf spot: Tan, circular spots appear on parsley aralia.

404 **Xanthomonas leaf spot:** Tan lesions with purple margins appear on Fabian aralia.

Pothos

405 **Rhizoctonia aerial blight:** Plants have large areas of black tissue decay, especially close to pot centers.

Pothos

406 Southern blight: Partially rotted leaves yellow, and potting medium surface has a white mycelial fan.

407 Nitrogen toxicity: Brown, dead areas appear in the white portions of leaves.

408 Compare nitrogen deficiency (left) and nitrogen toxicity (right) to appropriate levels of nitrogen (center).

409 Pythium root rot: Lower foliage yellows and wilts.

410 Pythium root rot: You can easily pull roots from the growing medium. Roots appear stringy due to cortical decay.

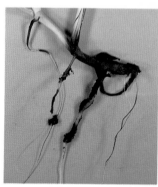

Primula

411 Pythium root rot: Plant wilts; root system turns brown and soft from decay.

412 Tomato spotted wilt virus: Leaves turn brown along veins, resembling spray injury.

413 Tomato spotted wilt virus: Leaves have severe yellow mottling.

Radermachera

414 **Corynespora leaf spot:** Large black lesions cause leaf abscission on China Doll.

415 **Bud mites:** New growth is severely distorted.

Ranunculus

416 **Powdery mildew:** White patches coalesce to cover leaf surfaces.

Saintpaulia

417 Botrytis blight: Plant center rots.

418 Botrytis blight: Flowers get blight, too.

419 Botrytis blight: Leaf lesions are brown and wedge-shaped.

420 **Phytophthora stem rot:** Lower leaves wilt and rot.

421 **Phytophthora petiole rot:** Closeup of lower leaf infected with Phytophthora.

422 **Phytophthora crown rot:** Young growth at the plant center turns brown.

Saintpaulia

423 **Foliar nematode:** New leaves are distorted and may show white color breaks.

424 **Foliar nematode:** New growth is stunted.

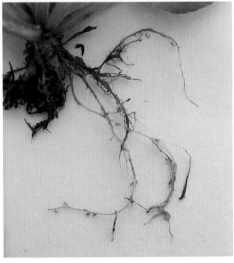

425 **Root knot nematode:** Galls appear along entire root length.

426 Powdery mildew: White spore masses show on leaf surfaces.

427 Ethylene: Severe water-soaking starts at the petiole and extends into leaf blades.

428 Ethylene: Injury occurs to tissue at the center of the flower.

Saintpaulia

429 Cold water: White rings appear on upper leaf surfaces.

430 Pythium root rot: Root systems turn brown and rot.

431 Ammonium toxicity: Leaves show interveinal yellowing.

432 Rhizoctonia stem rot: Plants wilt.

433 Rhizoctonia rot: Brown cankers form at petiole bases.

434 **Rhizoctonia crown rot:** Cobwebby fungal growth may appear at the soil surface under high humidity.

435 **Cylindrocarpon stem rot:** Brown cankers form at petiole bases.

436 **Tomato spotted wilt virus:** Brown lines appear in concentric patterns near petiole.

437 Corynespora leaf spot: Large, black lesions appear on leaf margins, especially those in contact with potting medium.

438 Cyclamen mite: New leaves are stunted, pale and hardened.

Salvia

439 **Corynespora leaf spot:** Black, circular spots can cause leaf drop.

440 **Rust:** Light green areas on upper leaf surface sometimes contain spore pustules.

441 **Rust:** Dark brown spore pustules are easily seen on lower leaf surfaces.

442 Alternaria leaf spot: Coalescence of black spots causes severe lower leaf loss.

443 Sweet potato whitefly: Whitefly feeding results in yellowing and distortion of new leaves.

Sansevieria

444 Chilling injury: Plants have white, sunken, soft tissue.

445 Stem rot: Black spore heads of the fungus Aspergillus may cover soft rot at cutting bases.

446 Fusarium stem rot: Plants have basal stem rot and leaf spot.

Schefflera

447 **Tomato spotted wilt virus:** Leaves have yellow ring spots.

448 **Pseudomonas leaf spot:** Black, wet spots with yellow halos form on leaf margins.

Schefflera

449 **Xanthomonas leaf spot:** Tan, roughly circular spots appear on leaves.

450 **Alternaria leaf spot:** Leaves have sunken, round, tan spots with yellow margins.

451 **Pythium root rot:** Lower leaves turn yellow and abscise.

452 **Bendiocarb damage:** Leaves show marginal browning following drenches with this insecticide.

Schefflera

453 Pythium damping-off: Seedlings
collapse at soil line or do not emerge.

454 Dodder (parasitic plant): Yellowish-orange wiry
growths appear on stems.

455 Frost injury: Affected foliage bronzes and dies; new growth shows some distortion.

456 Xanthomonas leaf spot: Brown spots are sometimes vein-delimited.

457 Xanthomonas leaf spot: Ghost-type spots are commonly confused with other problems.

Schefflera

458 Pseudomonas leaf spot: Dead, brown areas run along veins.

459 Rhizoctonia damping-off: Seedling collapse is easily confused with Pythium damping-off.

460 Alternaria leaf spot: Spots are black with a bright yellow halo and sometimes expand up to 3 inches.

461 Two-spotted spider mite: Large areas of necrosis occur due to desiccation.

Snapdragon

462 **Pythium root rot:** Stunting and grayish, off-color foliage accompany root rot.

463 **Botrytis blight:** Stem cankers cause wilt.

464 Downy mildew: Gray, fuzzy, sporulation appears on leaf undersides.

465 Powdery mildew: White patches appear on upper leaf surfaces.

466 Rust: Pale spots appear on upper leaf surfaces and dark brown spore pustules on leaf undersides.

Spathiphyllum

467 Excess fertilizer: Leaves show marginal browning.

468 Magnesium deficiency: Outer leaf margins yellow and tissue disintegrates.

469 Erwinia rot: Black, mushy rot results in spadix disintegration.

470 Benomyl
phytotoxicity:
Outer leaf
margins discolor
following drench
applications of
excessive rates.

471 Myrothecium leaf spot: Leaves have circular
spots with bright yellow halos.

Spathiphyllum

472 Myrothecium petiole rot: Small tissue-cultured plantlets show petiole rot.

473 Phytophthora leaf spot: Large black spots form on leaf edges during summer.

474 Cylindrocladium leaf spot: Large black spots with bright yellow halos are common.

475 Cylindrocladium root and petiole and root rot: Root systems may be completely lost.

476 Cylindrocladium root and petiole and root rot: Lower leaves wilt, turn yellow and die.

Syngonium

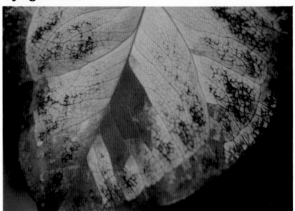

477 Xanthomonas blight: Water-soaked, slightly yellow lesions confined between veins are an early symptom.

478 Xanthomonas blight: Lesions turn brown and dry.

479 Xanthomonas blight: Spots can be vein-delimited or marginal.

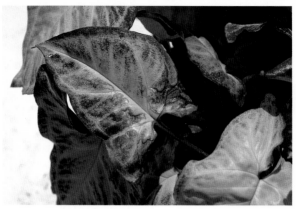

480 Copper toxicity: Dry, irregularly-shaped spots start as water-soaked lesions similar to those caused by Xanthomonas.

481 Erwinia blight: Leaves have concentric rings of expansion with spots rarely confined between veins.

482 Myrothecium leaf spot: Small tissue-cultured plants can be killed when spots form on their leaves.

Syngonium

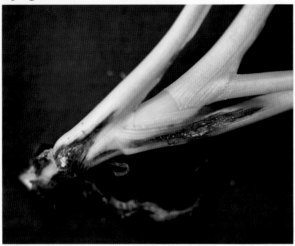

483 Black cane rot: Plants show reddish streaks from cutting bases and black fungal growth.

Tulip

484 Botrytis blight: Petals have lesions.

485 Botrytis blight or fire: Lower leaves have a burned appearance.

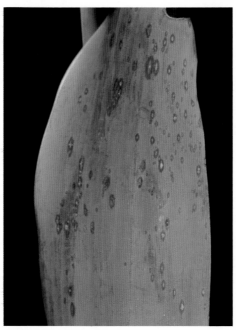

486 Botrytis blight or fire: Elliptical tan leaf spots closeup.

Tulip

487 **Botrytis blight or fire:** Sporulation closeup.

Verbena

488 **Powdery mildew:** Leaves have purple patches on upper surfaces and mildew colonies on undersides.

489 **Pythium damping-off:** Root infection causes stunting and collapse of young plants.

Vinca

490 **Ulocladium leaf spot:** Spots form all over leaves and cause overall plant yellowing.

491 **Phytophthora stem rot:** Symptoms are similar to those caused by Rhizoctonia.

Vinca

492 Rhizopus stem rot: Affected branches wilt and collapse.

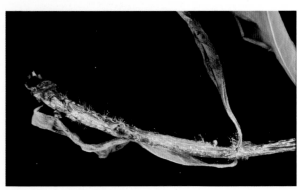

493 Rhizopus stem rot: Cankered stem may show sporulation.

494 Rhizoctonia stem rot: Lower leaves wilt and die due to stem cankers.

495 Rhizoctonia damping-off: Brown, constricted cankers appear at the soil line.

496 Rhizoctonia damping off: The fungus can girdle young seedlings at the soil line.

497 Thielaviopsis root rot: Foliage yellowing accompanies black root rot.

Viola

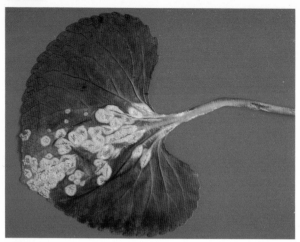

498 Rust: Upper leaf surfaces of violets show pustules in yellow spots.

Xanthosoma

499 Myrothecium leaf spot: Damping-off can occur when spots form on small seedlings.

500 **Myrothecium leaf spot:** Leaves can have large lesions with chlorotic halos.

Zinnia

501 **Powdery mildew:** White fungus colonies appear on upper leaf surfaces.

502 **Bacterial leaf spot:** Leaves have yellow-rimmed, angular spots, tan to purple in color.

Zinnia

503 Alternaria leaf spot: Tan lesions have a purplish border and coalesce to destroy large portions of the plant.

504 Alternaria leaf spot: Petal lesions are black on Z. *linearis*.

505 **Alternaria leaf spot:** Petal lesions turn tan.

506 **Botrytis blight:** Lower leaf infection may lead to a stem canker at the base of the plant.

Glossary

Angular leaf spot A spot with straight sides, bounded by veins; not round.

Anthracnose fungi Those fungi producing their spores in an acervulus (one of several container types for fungal spores).

Blight Extensive necrosis; infection is not localized, but spreads rapidly under favorable conditions.

Callus Undifferentiated cells produced at a wound site.

Canker A dead area on a stem or branch.

Chlorotic Pale or yellow, lacking the normal amount of chlorophyll.

Color breaking Interruption of the normal petal color by darker or lighter streaks due to viral infection.

Cortical Referring to the root cortex; the softer tissue surrounding the central vascular tissue.

Damping-off Seedling collapse and death due to fungal infection.

Desiccation Drying out.

Gall Swollen plant part.

Leaf abscission Leaf drop.

Lesion A dead area within healthy plant tissue.

Mosaic A symptom induced by viral infection; a pattern of distinct patches of yellow within a leaf.

Mottle A symptom induced by viral infection; appearance similar to a mosaic, but with a less distinct demarcation between yellow and green areas.

Mycelia The vegetative body of fungi composed of a network of many individual strands.

Necrotic, necrosis Describes dead plant tissue; such areas turn brown or black and may become dry and papery with time.

Oedema Blisters on (primarily) the leaf undersides caused by physiological stress.

Parasitizing Using another organism as a food source.

Pathogen A microorganism that causes a contagious plant disease.

Pedicel Flower stem.

Petiole Leaf stem.

Phytotoxicity The potential for plant injury from a pesticide application.

Pustule Fruiting structure of a rust fungus.

Pycnidia Fungal spore containers.

Ring spot A virus-induced symptom; a spot formed by several concentric rings in a color that contrasts with healthy leaf tissue; rings are usually yellow or brown and may resemble fingerprints.

Sclerotia Resistant structures allowing survival in a dormant condition in soil; formed by some fungi.

Senescent Plant tissues in a natural state of decline due to aging.

Soft rot Decay of plant tissue caused by a pathogen.

Spadix The spike portion of flowers in the Araceae family (such as anthurium).

Spore The propagative unit for fungi; produced either asexually or sexually.

Sporodochia Fungal spore structures.

Sporulation Spore production by a fungus.

Systemic infection An infection that isn't localized and that includes invasion of xylem and/or phloem.

Vascular infection An infection of the xylem vessels; interferes with water transport.

Vein-delimited The leaf veins form the boundary of the affected areas.

Veinal necrosis Portions of veins are darkly discolored and dysfunctional.

Virescent Abnormally green; used to describe tissue that is normally bright colored, such as petals.

Water-soaking The dark, greasy and wet appearance of certain infected areas.

Yellow halo A pale to yellow area surrounding a lesion.

Zonate lesion Lesion with a target-like pattern of concentric outlines within it.

References

In order to learn more about any particular disease illustrated here, consult additional sources for detailed information. A wide range of materials is available, no one of them serving to answer all questions you might have. On foliage plant diseases, *The Compendium of Ornamental Foliage Plant Diseases* by A.R. Chase (APS Press) will provide additional information. Diseases of flowering crops are covered extensively in a two-book set edited by David Strider, *Diseases of Floral Crops* (Praeger Press). *The Compendium of Rose Diseases* edited by R.K. Horst, *Compendium of Rhododendron and Azalea Diseases*, edited by D.L. Coyier and M.K. Roane, and *Diseases and Disorders of Ornamental Palms* by A.R. Chase and T.K. Broschat (APS Press) provide in-depth treatment on those crops. Other flower crop compendia are currently in preparation. Additional general plant disease references with descriptions of disease problems are *Westcott's Plant Disease Handbook* revised by R.K. Horst (Van Nostrand Reinhold), *Diseases of Ornamental Plants* by J.L. Forsberg (University of Illinois Press), *Diseases and Pests of Ornamental Plants* by P.P. Pirone (Wiley-Interscience) and *Ball Pest and Disease Manual* by Charles C. Powell and Richard K. Lindquist (Ball Publishing). The Cooperative Extension Service of your state can provide you with additional helpful publications.

About the authors

Margery Daughtrey has 14 years of experience as a plant pathologist specializing in ornamental plant diseases. She is a Senior Extension Associate with the Department of Plant Pathology of Cornell University, stationed at the Long Island Horticultural Research Laboratory in Riverhead, New York. Margery has a bachelor's degree in biology from the College of William and Mary, and a master's in plant pathology from the University of Massachusetts. Her extension education program focuses on teaching effective disease management for greenhouse and nursery crops and landscape ornamentals.

Margery has first-hand familiarity with proper identification through the ornamental plant disease diagnostic lab she directs on Long Island. She also conducts research on disease management and has participated in many local and national programs on disease avoidance.

Ann Chase, a native Californian, has a doctorate in plant pathology from the University of California at Riverside. Ann started at the Central Florida Research and Education Center in

1979 after completing her dissertation on a vascular disease of Shasta daisy. Research efforts during the first few years at Apopka included describing new diseases caused by both fungal and bacterial plant pathogens, completing a project to release tissue-cultured Perfection 137B dieffen-bachias and developing the fungicide Terraguard 50WP label. Her ultimate research goal is presenting an integrated approach to controlling bacterial diseases that employs both chemical and nutritional aspects.

Ann has also prepared a *Compendium of Ornamental Foliage Plant Diseases* with the American Phytopathological Society, published chapters in several books and developed slide sets on foliage plant diseases. She continues to publish articles on a wide variety of topics for both scientific journals and popular magazines and speaks at local and national conferences.

After viewing one of Margery or Ann's presentations, growers often come up to them and request copies of slides used to take back to their operations for reference, as well as to share with others. This book is, in part, a response to the interest for in-house visual aids that so many growers have expressed over the years.

Index (by photo number)

Nitrogen deficiency 15, 27, 408
Nitrogen toxicity 190, 407
Nutritional or root rot problem 165
Odontoglossum ringspot virus (ORSV) 344
Oedema 260
Oidium begoniae 37, 38, 39
Oidium spp. 101, 102, 416, 426, 465, 488
Peronospora antirrhini 464
Phomopsis spp. 174, 199, 200
Phyllosticta draconis 109, 110
Phyllostictina sp. 353
Phytophthora parasitica 20, 21, 26, 275, 356, 398, 399, 400, 420, 421, 422, 491
Phytophthora parasitica var. *nicotianae* 366
Phytophthora spp. 173, 323, 473
Powdery mildew 37, 38, 39, 101, 102, 266, 319, 320, 416, 426, 465, 488, 501
Pseudomonas andropogonis 46
Pseudomonas cichorii 75, 76, 77, 78, 79, 80, 186, 204, 223, 268, 288, 403, 448, 458
Pseudomonas gladioli 191, 192, 193
Pseudomonas spp. 64
Pseudomonas syringae 1, 289, 294, 295
Puccinia antirrhini 466
Puccinia horiana 81, 82
Puccinia pelargonii-zonalis 254, 255, 256, 257
Pucciniastrum pustulatum 215, 216, 217
Puccinia tanaceti 83, 84, 85
Pythium and fungus gnat larvae 243
Pythium spp. 4, 5, 11, 22, 47, 151, 245, 246, 247, 264, 279, 299, 326, 333, 341, 354, 394, 395, 409, 410, 411, 430, 451, 453, 462, 489
Rhizoctonia spp. 6, 107, 143, 187, 188, 189, 237, 238, 280, 281, 292, 293, 298, 316, 325, 355, 360, 361, 364, 365, 372, 383, 384, 405, 432, 433, 434, 459, 494, 495, 496
Rhizopus stolonifer 176, 253, 269, 270, 271, 317, 318, 385, 386, 492, 493
Rhodococcus fascians 224
Rust (see also *Coleosporium, Puccinia, Pucciniastrum*) 141, 142, 440, 441, 498

Sclerotinia sclerotiorum 90, 339, 359
Sclerotinia sp. 329
Sclerotium rolfsii 112, 197, 198, 367, 406
Smut 66, 133, 134
Soluble salts, excess 65, 259
Speckling 169
Sphaceloma poinsettiae 375, 376, 377
Sphaerotheca humili f. sp. *fuliginea* 319, 320
Streptomycin sulfate phytotoxicity 283
Sunburn 152
Sweet potato whitefly 443
Thielaviopsis basicola 115, 218, 219, 220, 346, 347, 387, 388, 497
Thrips 261
Tomato spotted wilt virus (TSWV) 17, 25, 40, 41, 42, 43, 44, 91, 92, 93, 95, 96, 97, 98, 99, 131, 132, 136, 180, 181, 182, 267, 276, 277, 278, 300, 301, 302, 303, 304, 305, 306, 307, 308, 309, 310, 311, 357, 412, 413, 436, 447
Two-spotted spider mite 461
Ulocladium sp. 490
Verticillium wilt 244
Virus (unidentified) 68, 258, 343, 350
Xanthomonas campestris pv. *begoniae* 33, 34, 35, 36
Xanthomonas campestris pv. *dieffenbachiae* 9, 23, 157, 363
Xanthomonas campestris pv. *fici* 203
Xanthomonas campestris pv. *hederae* 185, 284, 404, 449, 456, 457
Xanthomonas campestris pv. *malvacearum* 290
Xanthomonas campestris pv. *pelargonii* 225, 226, 227, 228, 229, 230, 231, 232, 233, 234, 235, 236
Xanthomonas campestris pv. *poinsetticola* 118, 119, 379
Xanthomonas campestris pv. unknown 209, 324, 348, 373, 374
Xanthomonas campestris pv. *vesicatoria* 358
Xanthomonas campestris pv. *zinniae* 502
Xanthomonas spp. 477, 478, 479